KT-555-522

BULLYING

by Karen Bryant-Mole

Consultant: John Hall,
Counselling Support Manager of ChildLine

Wayland

KIRKCALDY DISTRICT LIBRARIES

036690

J371.58/BRY

TC

Designed by Helen White
Edited by Deb Elliott

We gratefully acknowledge the assistance of the following people
in the production of this book:
Janice Green, Anti-Bullying Campaign
Dr Rachel Waugh, Principal Clinical Psychologist,
Great Ormond Street Hospital

All the words in **bold** are explained in the glossary on page 31.

First published in 1992 by Wayland (Publishers) Limited
61 Western Road, Hove, East Sussex BN3 1JD

© Copyright Wayland (Publishers) Limited

British Library Cataloguing in Publication Data
Bryant – Mole, Karen
  Bullying. – (What's Happening? Series)
  I. Title II. Series
  371.5

ISBN 0 7502 0443 5

Phototypeset by White Design
Printed and bound in Belgium by Casterman S.A.

CONTENTS

WHAT IS BULLYING?

RIGHT Mark says: 'It's when someone punches you for no reason.

LEFT Nina says: 'It's people saying horrible things about you.'

'Bullying' is a difficult word because it can mean lots of different things. Mark said it was someone punching you. The sort of bullying when someone actually touches you is called **physical bullying**. It doesn't have to be a punch. It could be something as small as someone always pulling your hair when they walk past you.

Nina said it was people saying horrible things about you. That sort of bullying is called **verbal bullying**. It means that the bully hurts you by the things he or she says.

LEFT Daniel says: 'It's when there's someone in the class that everyone else is frightened of.'

Daniel described bullying not as an action but as a feeling. He said that everyone feels frightened of a bully.

Perhaps it would be best to think of bullying as being both the way the bully acts and the way the person who is being bullied feels. A good description of bullying might be this: anything that a person does on purpose because he or she knows it will upset another person.

WHY DO PEOPLE BULLY?

BELOW Sasha bullied other children because she felt her parents weren't really bothered about her.

Sasha used to bully other children. She now thinks that the reason she used to be a bully was because she felt that no one was interested in her. Her mum and dad were so busy it seemed they hardly ever had a moment to talk to her. Sometimes she felt she might as well be invisible. Being a bully was Sasha's way of getting other people to notice her.

LEFT Jason used to be a bully because it made him feel important.

Jason used to be a bully too. *'I was useless at everything at school. Then I found there was something that I was good at – bullying. I stopped bullying when I changed schools, partly because I wasn't one of the biggest any more and partly because the teachers there didn't make me feel stupid like they did at the other school.'*

There are lots of other reasons why children bully. Sometimes it is because bullying makes them feel powerful, or because they don't know how to make friends. Sometimes they bully because they have been bullied themselves.

Almost all the children who are bullies are unhappy. They might not look unhappy to you. In fact they might even laugh and joke about bullying, but deep inside they are probably unhappy.

WHO GETS BULLIED?

ABOVE The bullies teased Zara by making her try to reach for the book.

Zara enjoyed school until some of the children in the class started picking on her. She was quite a bit smaller than most of the other children and some of them had started calling her names. They took things from her and held them up high, knowing she couldn't reach them.

Bullies often look for something different about another child and then use that as an excuse for bullying them. Zara was bullied about her size. Someone else might be bullied about the colour of their skin or about their clothes.

Using something that is different about a person as a way of bullying them is very mean. If you were the smallest in your class, how would you feel if someone kept going on about it?

It might not be easy but if you are being bullied like this, try to **ignore** it. If the bullies see that they can make you cry or make you cross they will keep on doing it. If you ignore them they may get fed up with trying to upset you and stop. If you find it too difficult to ignore the bullying and you can't help getting upset, tell an adult about it. Just talking about it can sometimes be helpful.

If the bullying is happening at school it is a good idea to tell a teacher. Even if ignoring the bullies works and they stop bullying you, they will probably try to upset someone else unless they are stopped.

BELOW Zara told her teacher how the bullying made her feel.

DO IT OR ELSE!

Sometimes bullies threaten other children by telling them that if they don't do a particular thing something dreadful will happen. That's what happened to Rob.

RIGHT Rob gave his dinner money to the bullies because he was scared.

'I bring dinner money to school every day. One day these two boys told me that if I didn't give them my dinner money they would smash the windows in my dad's shop. I didn't know what to do. If I didn't give them the money and they really did break my dad's windows, it would be all my fault. So I gave them the money. I had to hide in the cloakroom when everyone else went to lunch.'

BELOW Rob had to hide himself away from everyone.

One lunchtime a teacher spotted Rob in the cloakroom and asked him what he was doing. The teacher was cross with him at first. But when she heard the whole story and realized that Rob really was frightened, she told him that she would try to sort it out.

She discovered that the boys had been taking money from other children too. The bullies thought that all the children would be too frightened to tell on them. Once the bullies realized that they had been found out they stopped doing it.

If you are ever bullied in this way the best thing to do is to tell an adult about it. It might be difficult but this is not a problem you can sort out by yourself.

IS IT MY FAULT?

Often children who are bullied think that it must be their fault. James felt like this. *'I've been bullied for as long as I can remember. I get picked on because I don't like playing football and I don't have the right clothes. There's loads of reasons. I'm not the same as them. I used to mind a lot at first, but then I suppose I got used to it. Now I just expect to get bullied. That way I don't get upset when it happens.'*

Have you ever squashed all the air out of a plastic ball and watched it spring out again? Being bullied can be a bit like that. When you are being bullied you feel as if all the happiness has been squashed out of you, but usually you manage to spring back again. If you keep on squashing the ball you can sometimes squash it so flat that it won't spring back.

James has been bullied for so long that he is well and truly squashed and has stopped even trying to spring back. He could try thinking of things he likes about himself and finding things that he is good at.

Once you begin to feel good about yourself it is easier to start springing back. He could also try to make friends with some of the other children in the class. Having friends helps you feel good about yourself too. Most importantly of all James must stop thinking that it is his fault that he is bullied.

OPPOSITE James had begun to believe what the bullies were saying about him.

TELL-TALE!

ABOVE A group of children said they wouldn't be friends with Kathryn any more.

Kathryn was being bullied. A group of children who used to be her friends refused to play with her any more and started saying horrible things about her. The first time it happened she told the teacher on playground duty. The teacher promised to watch out. The trouble was that because the other children weren't actually doing anything to Kathryn there wasn't anything for the teacher to see. In the end the teacher got so fed up with her always complaining that she told Kathryn not to be so silly and to stop telling tales.

Kathryn wasn't being silly. The other children really were upsetting her. Thinking that there was nothing she could do about it made her feel very lonely.

Kathryn had tried telling one adult. That hadn't worked but perhaps a different adult might be able to help. Kathryn could tell another teacher about it. One who she thinks would understand how miserable the bullying was making her.

She should tell her mum or dad about it too. Talking about it might help and if Kathryn couldn't get any of the teachers to take the bullying seriously then her parents might want to talk to them. Sometimes adults only believe other adults.

Kathryn decided to tell her class teacher about the bullying. He was very unhappy about it and got all the children involved together to talk about how they would feel if they were being picked on. Once they thought about it like that, the bullying stopped.

BELOW When they talked about the bullying with their teacher, the other children realized they wouldn't like it if the same thing happened to them.

BOARDING SCHOOL BULLIES

Most children who are being bullied can at least feel safe in their own homes. For some children the bullying may never stop.

George had been at **boarding school** for almost a year and was being bullied by some of the older boys. When he told his parents about it his dad just laughed and said that he remembered being bullied at school too. He told George not to be a baby and said that it would stop when he moved into the second year.

George felt really miserable. He couldn't get away from the bullying. His parents didn't even take the problem seriously. If anything they seemed to expect it.

At George's school all the boys have one special teacher who they can talk to about **problems**. George's teacher was Mr Ellis. George didn't really want to talk to him about the bullying in case the bullies found out, but eventually he decided it was his only hope. Mr Ellis was very concerned. George told him when and how he was being bullied. Mr Ellis made it look as if he just happened to be in the right place at the right time and caught the bullies at it. He was able to deal with the bullying in a way that didn't make it look as though it was George who had told on them.

OPPOSITE Boarding schools shouldn't just look after your education, they should look after you as a person.

BELOW Bullying should never be thought of as part of boarding school life.

ADULT BULLIES

Most bullied children are bullied by other children. Some children, though, are bullied by adults.

Lorna is very good at maths, English and science. Mrs Bentley used to tell her how well she was doing but when she moved classes everything changed. Mrs Langley called Lorna 'Miss Clever Clogs' and she seemed pleased whenever Lorna made any mistakes. Lorna wasn't very good at sport. In one PE lesson Mrs Langley asked Lorna to show the others how to do a handstand. Then she told everyone it was the worst handstand she had ever seen. Lorna was very unhappy.

BELOW
Sometimes Mrs Langley made all the other children laugh at Lorna.

LEFT Lorna's parents talked to the head teacher about the bullying.

Lorna told her parents and they spoke to Mrs Langley but she just said that Lorna was imagining things. When it continued Lorna's parents went to see the head teacher. He spoke to Mrs Langley but she again said that it was Lorna's imagination. Lorna felt helpless. It was her word against a teacher's and everyone believed the teacher.

Her parents decided to keep a **diary** of all the things that happened. Every day Lorna told them if she had been bullied and what had been said. Lorna's parents went back to the head teacher and showed him the diary. He realized that these were not the kind of things a child would make up and he told Mrs Langley to stop behaving towards Lorna in this way.

Bullying by an adult usually needs another adult to sort things out. You might find that no one takes you seriously at first. Try keeping a diary of exactly what happens. It may help to prove to another adult that there really is a problem.

FRIEND OR BULLY?

ABOVE *At first Sam enjoyed being part of the gang.*

Sometimes bullying isn't about what other people do to you. It can be about what other people make you do.

Sam got on well with all the children in his class but was particularly friendly with three boys. One of the boys, Lee, thought it would be a great idea to form a **gang**. It was fun being part of a gang. One day Lee came into school with some sweets which he shared with the others. Then he told the others that he had stolen the sweets and that unless they stole something too they couldn't be part of the gang any more.

Sam knew it was wrong to steal but he wanted to be part of the gang. He couldn't decide what to do. His mum sensed that something was wrong and persuaded Sam to talk to her about it.

Even though he trusted his mum he didn't want to tell her who the other children were. So Sam's mum asked him to think about whether he really wanted to be friends with children who might get him into serious trouble.

Sam decided that friends like Lee really weren't worth having and he refused to steal anything. He stopped playing with Lee and the others and spent more time with his other friends in the class.

If someone says that they will only be your friend if you do something you don't want to, try to say no.

BELOW Sam realized that Lee was not a true friend. A true friend would never make you do something you didn't want to do. Sam decided to spend more time with his other friends.

MATTHEW

Sometimes children who have been bullied become bullies themselves.

Matthew is a bully. He picks on younger children. Everyone who is smaller than Matthew is frightened of him. He is the youngest in a family of three boys. He is bullied at home by his older brothers. If they want something that Matthew has they just push him out of the way and take it. Sometimes they punch and kick him for no reason at all.

BELOW Matthew bullies younger children.

His brothers' behaviour has taught Matthew that to get what you want you have to be rough. Now he picks on children who are smaller than him in the same way that his older brothers pick on him.

Matthew's bullying got so bad that he was sent to the head teacher nearly every day. When the head saw that simply punishing Matthew wasn't having any effect she decided

ABOVE *Matthew is bullied at home by his brothers.*

to try something else. She encouraged Matthew to talk about why he was bullying and how it felt to be bullied. Matthew said he did feel bad about bullying and that sometimes he felt very lonely.

The head suggested that if Matthew tried to make friends with the younger children he might find that being liked by someone is a much better feeling than being feared by them. She also promised to speak with Matthew's parents to see if there was anything she could do to help with the bullying at home.

IT'S NOT MY PROBLEM

ABOVE Lisa had seen other children being bullied. She didn't think it was anything to do with her.

It can be very easy to think that because you are not being bullied it is not your problem.

There are two girls in Lisa's school who are bullies. Although Lisa has never been bullied by them she has seen them bullying other children. Because it is happening to someone else she doesn't think it is anything to do with her. She even feels lucky that it is someone else's problem.

It is easy to understand why Lisa feels like this. But if you think about it carefully you might decide that it isn't very helpful. Seeing someone else being bullied and feeling pleased that it isn't you is rather **selfish**. You wouldn't like it if you were being bullied and everyone else ignored it.

By ignoring the bullying you are letting the bully think that it is all right to behave like this. And even though you might think that you are not affected by the bullying, you probably are.

Part of the reason that Lisa was never bullied was because she always stayed with a large group of friends. They tried to keep away from the two bullies and made sure that they didn't do things which would annoy them. In fact, they used to be especially nice to the bullies. Although Lisa wasn't being bullied, the bullies were making her behave in a particular way.

BELOW Bullying affects everyone. Don't let the bullies get away with it.

WHAT CAN YOU DO?

Bullies make it clear to the children they bully that if they tell anyone about it the bullying will get worse. The children are then too frightened to do or say anything. As telling is really the only effective way to stop bullying, one of the most important things a school can do is to make it safe to tell about bullying.

You don't have to be bullied to want the bullying stopped. Lisa and her friends got fed up with the behaviour of the other two girls. They asked their teacher if they could have a class **discussion** about bullying and it soon became clear that no one in the class liked the bullying. Once the bullied children felt

BELOW Lisa thought a class discussion about bullying might be helpful.

that the rest of the class supported them, they were able to talk about what was happening and how they felt about it.

Bullies work by picking on one or two children at a time. If they know that the other children in the class will not let them do this they are powerless.

Lisa's class drew up a set of rules about bullying. One of the rules was that anyone who was being bullied should be able to talk to a teacher and know that they will be taken seriously. Another was that the other children in the class would help anyone who was being bullied.

Lisa's class felt this was so important that they held an assembly all about bullying. The other classes started discussing it too and eventually the whole school developed a plan for dealing with bullies.

ABOVE The class thought about ways of stopping the bullying.

TELLING

ABOVE *Louise was bullied by her older sisters. She didn't know who to turn to for help.*

If you are being bullied, the first message is tell, tell, tell. Telling is not always easy, though. You might be frightened that telling will make the bullying worse.

You could ask the person you talk to to help you in such a way that the bullies don't know that it is you that told on them. If you tell a teacher, perhaps the teacher could have a general discussion about bullying with the whole class. Or perhaps your teacher could make it look as though he or she just happens to be in the right place at the right time and sees the bullying.

You might find that the adult you tell can't, or won't, help you. That will probably make you feel even more lonely and miserable, but don't give up. Try someone else. Think of someone who will understand how you feel.

Do tell your parents about it too. It might be easier for a teacher to actually do something about the bullying if it is happening in school time but your mum or dad will probably be good listeners. They might be able to give you some helpful advice and telling them about the bullying may stop you feeling quite so alone with the problem.

It can be difficult to stop bullying but it is not impossible. Sometimes adults say that being bullied is just part of growing up – this is not true. No one should have to put up with being bullied.

RIGHT *Joe was picked on by other boys in his school. He didn't know why they did it so he blamed himself. It was not his fault. No one deserves to be bullied.*

BELOW *Being bullied can make you feel very lonely and confused. It must be stopped. Please tell someone.*

FOR PARENTS AND TEACHERS

Sometimes children who are being bullied are too frightened to talk to their teachers or even to their parents. It is perhaps worth mentioning some of the signs that *may* indicate that a child is being bullied.

Children who are being bullied may
- be reluctant to go to school.
- start performing badly at school.
- lose their appetites.
- cry in their sleep.
- have nightmares.
- come home with torn clothing or missing possessions but be unable to give plausible accounts of what has happened.

If a child does talk to you about being bullied, do take him or her seriously. Children who are being bullied are likely to feel lonely, vulnerable and powerless. They need your support.

GLOSSARY

Boarding school   A school where pupils live and sleep during the school term.

Diary   A book in which you can write all the things that happen during the day.

Discussion   When a group of people get together and talk about a particular subject.

Gang   A group of people who go about together.

Ignore   To take no notice of something.

Physical bullying   Bullying someone by kicking, punching or hitting them.

Problems   Things that make you worried or unhappy.

Selfish   Thinking only about yourself and not about other people.

Verbal bullying   Bullying someone by saying horrible and nasty things to them and about them.

BOOKS TO READ

Bullying by Angela Grunsell (Gloucester Press, 1989)
Health and Friends by Dorothy Baldwin (Wayland, 1987)
Racism by Angela Grunsell (Gloucester Press, 1990)
Your Friends by Michael Pollard (Wayland, 1989)

INDEX

Picture Acknowledgements

The following pictures are from: Cephas Picture Library cover, 4 (bottom, Chris Gander), 29 (bottom, Stephen Bryan); Chris Fairclough 28; Jeff Greenberg 6, 8, 9, 13, 14, 15, 20, 21, 24, 25, 26, 27, 29 (top); Zul Mukhida/Chapel Studios 10, 11, 16, 17, 18, 19, 22, 23; Tony Stone 5 (Paul McKelvey); Wayland Picture Library 4 (top), 7.

Some of the people who are featured in this book are models. We gratefully acknowledge the help and assistance of all those individuals who have been involved in this project. We would like to extend a special thanks to Mr John Hastwell and the pupils of Burwash Church of England School, East Sussex.